CALEB MAINA IDI

SYRIA-PALESTINE WARCRAFT

ROOTS OF GLOBAL UNREST AND INSTABILITY

SYRIA-PALESTINE WARCRAFT
ROOTS OF GLOBAL UNREST AND INSTABILITY

TABLE OF CONTENTS

- The status of Palestinian statehood and recognition
- The applicability of international humanitarian law and human rights law

Chapter 4: Humanitarian Impacts of the Conflict
- Displacement and refugee crises in Syria and Palestine
- The impact of violence on civilians
- The role of humanitarian organizations and aid efforts

Chapter 5: Prospects for Peace and Reconciliation
- Lessons from successful peace processes in other conflicts
- The potential for a two-state solution
- The role of civil society and grassroots initiatives
- Conclusion
- Summary of key findings
- Implications and recommendations for policymakers and practitioners
- Future research directions.
- **REFERENCES**

Arab-Israeli Conflict Overview

Introduction

The Arab-Israeli conflict is one of the most enduring and complex conflicts in modern history. The conflict has been ongoing for over a century and has involved multiple parties, including the Israelis, Palestinians, and other Arab states. The roots of the conflict can be traced back to the early 20th century, with the emergence of Zionism and the displacement of Palestinian Arabs. The conflict has evolved over time, with the emergence of new players and shifting alliances. This book seeks to provide an overview of the historical roots of the conflict, as well as its current status and future prospects.

Background and Context of the Conflict

The roots of the Arab-Israeli conflict can be traced back to the late 19th century, with the emergence of the Zionist movement. Zionism was a political movement that aimed to establish a Jewish homeland in Palestine, which was then part of the Ottoman Empire. The Zionist movement gained momentum in the early 20th century, with the support of the British government. In 1917, the British government issued the Balfour Declaration, which pledged support for the establishment of a Jewish homeland in Palestine.

The British government was motivated by a number of factors, including strategic interests in the region and a desire to win the support of Jewish communities around the world. However, the Balfour Declaration was also seen as a betrayal by the Arab population of Palestine, who had been promised independence by the British in return for their support during World War I. The Arab population saw the establishment of a Jewish homeland as a direct threat to their own interests, and tensions between Jews and Arabs began to escalate.

Objectives and Scope of the Book

The objective of this book is to provide an overview of the historical roots of the Arab-Israeli conflict, as well as its current status and future prospects. The book will focus on key events and turning points in the conflict, including the British mandate period, the displacement of Palestinian Arabs, the Arab-Israeli wars, and the involvement of other Arab states.

The scope of the book will be broad, encompassing a range of perspectives and viewpoints. The book will explore the experiences and perspectives of Jews, Arabs, and other parties involved in the conflict. It will also consider the impact of the conflict on the wider region and on international relations.

Methodology and Approach

The book will employ a range of methodologies and approaches, drawing on a variety of primary and secondary sources. These sources will include historical documents, academic studies, news reports, and personal accounts.

The book will adopt a critical and balanced approach, seeking to provide a comprehensive overview of the conflict that takes into account the perspectives and experiences of all parties involved. The book will also seek to provide an analysis of the underlying causes and drivers of the conflict, as well as its potential solutions.

Chapter 1
Historical Roots of the Conflict

Early Arab-Jewish Tensions and Conflicts in Palestine:

The early 20th century saw the emergence of tensions and conflicts between the Arab and Jewish communities in Palestine. These tensions were rooted in a number of factors, including conflicting national aspirations, competition for land and resources, and religious differences.

One of the key flashpoints in the early years of the conflict was the issue of Jewish immigration to Palestine. Jewish immigration began in the late 19th century, and by the early 20th century, Jews had established a significant presence in the region. Arab leaders were concerned about the impact of Jewish immigration on their own aspirations for self-determination, as well as the impact on Arab land and resources.

In 1920, violence erupted in Jerusalem between Jewish and Arab communities, leading to the deaths of several people. This was followed by a series of riots and attacks in other parts of Palestine, which left hundreds dead and thousands injured. The violence was fuelled by a number of factors, including economic competition between Jews and Arabs, as well as tensions over control of religious sites in Jerusalem.

British Mandate and the Emergence of Zionism:

In 1922, Palestine came under British control following the collapse of the Ottoman Empire. The British government had pledged to support the establishment of a Jewish homeland in Palestine, and they set about implementing policies to support Jewish immigration and settlement in the region.

The British mandate period saw a significant increase in Jewish immigration to Palestine, with many Jews fleeing persecution in Europe. This led to tensions with the Arab population, who saw the influx of Jewish settlers as a direct threat to their own aspirations for self-determination.

The emergence of Zionism as a political movement also played a significant role in the early years of the conflict. Zionism aimed to establish a Jewish homeland in Palestine, and it gained support from Jewish communities around the world. However, the Zionist movement was seen as a threat by the Arab population of Palestine, who saw the establishment of a Jewish state as a direct threat to their own interests.

Palestinian Displacement and the Arab-Israeli Wars:

The displacement of Palestinian Arabs is one of the key drivers of the Arab-Israeli conflict. During the 1948 Arab-Israeli War, around 700,000 Palestinian Arabs were forced to flee their homes, and many were never able to return. This event is known as the Nakba, or catastrophe, in Palestinian history.

The Arab-Israeli wars have been a significant factor in the ongoing conflict. The 1948 war saw the establishment of the State of Israel, which was recognized by the international community. However, the war also led to the displacement of hundreds of thousands of Palestinians, and it set the stage for further conflict in the years to come.

The 1967 Six-Day War was another key turning point in the conflict. Israel emerged victorious from the war, and it gained control of the West Bank, Gaza Strip, Sinai Peninsula, and Golan Heights. The war also marked the beginning of the occupation of the West Bank and Gaza Strip, which continues to this day.

Syrian Involvement and the Golan Heights Issue:

The involvement of other Arab states has also played a significant role in the Arab-Israeli conflict. Syria has been one of the key players in the conflict, particularly with regard to the issue of the Golan Heights.

The Golan Heights is a strategic plateau in southwestern Syria, which was captured by Israel during the 1967 Six-Day War. The area has been a point of contention between Israel and Syria ever since, with Syria demanding its return and Israel insisting on its right to hold onto the territory for security reasons.

The issue of the Golan Heights remains unresolved, and it continues to be a major point of tension between Israel and Syria. The conflict in Syria has also added a new dimension to the issue, with Israeli involvement in the Syrian conflict further complicating the situation.

The Arab-Israeli conflict is one of the most enduring and complex conflicts in modern history. The roots of the conflict can be traced back to the early 20th century, with the emergence of Zionism and the displacement of Palestinian Arabs. The conflict has evolved over time, with the involvement of new players and shifting alliances.

The conflict has had a profound impact on the region, and it continues to be a major point of tension in international relations. The resolution of the conflict remains a challenge, but it is essential for the achievement of lasting peace and stability in the region.

Chapter 2
Contemporary Developments in the Conflict

The world has seen some significant developments in the ongoing conflict in the Middle East over the past decade. The Syrian Civil War and its impact on the conflict, the Israeli-Palestinian peace process and its failures, the rise of Hamas and Hezbollah, and the role of external actors, including the United States and Russia, are some of the most important contemporary developments that have influenced the conflict.

The Syrian Civil War, which began in 2011, has had a significant impact on the region's conflict. What started as peaceful protests against the Assad regime quickly turned into a violent conflict that has resulted in the deaths of hundreds of thousands of people and displaced millions. The war has also allowed the rise of extremist groups, such as ISIS and Al Qaeda, which have further destabilized the region. The conflict has also drawn in external actors, including Russia, Iran, and Turkey, who have all supported different factions within Syria, further complicating the situation.

The Israeli-Palestinian peace process has been a long-standing issue in the region, with many failed attempts at finding a solution. Despite numerous rounds of negotiations, the conflict remains unresolved, with both sides unable to come to an agreement. The failure of the peace process has led to an increase in violence and tension, with frequent outbreaks of violence and clashes between Israelis and Palestinians.

The rise of Hamas and Hezbollah, two militant groups in the region, has further complicated the conflict. Both groups have engaged in violence against Israel and have used terrorism as a tactic. Their actions have led to increased tensions in the region, with Israel responding with military force, resulting in civilian casualties on both sides.

External actors, including the United States and Russia, have also played a significant role in the conflict. The United States has historically been a strong supporter of Israel, while Russia has supported Syria and Iran. Both countries have used their influence to support their respective allies, further fueling the conflict. The involvement of external actors has also made finding a solution to the conflict more challenging, as it has created competing interests and agendas.

In conclusion, the ongoing conflict in the Middle East has been shaped by various contemporary developments, including the Syrian Civil War, the failure of the Israeli-Palestinian peace process, the rise of Hamas and Hezbollah, and the role of external actors. These developments have made finding a solution to the conflict more challenging, and it will require a concerted effort from all parties involved to bring about a lasting peace.

Chapter 3
International Law and the Conflict

The Israeli-Palestinian conflict has been ongoing for decades, with numerous international efforts to resolve the issue. At the core of the conflict is the issue of Israeli settlements in the West Bank and East Jerusalem, which has been a major point of contention in international law. This chapter explores the legality of Israeli settlements in the West Bank and East Jerusalem, the status of Palestinian statehood and recognition, and the applicability of international humanitarian law and human rights law.

The Legality of Israeli Settlements in the West Bank and East Jerusalem

The West Bank and East Jerusalem were captured by Israel during the 1967 Six-Day War. Since then, Israel has built settlements in these territories, which has been a major source of tension in the Israeli-Palestinian conflict. The international community, including the United Nations, considers Israeli settlements in the West Bank and East Jerusalem to be illegal under international law.

The basis for this argument is the Fourth Geneva Convention of 1949, which prohibits an occupying power from transferring its civilian population into the territory it occupies. The International Court of Justice (ICJ) has also affirmed that the construction of Israeli settlements in the occupied Palestinian territory, including East Jerusalem, violates international humanitarian law.

Despite this, Israel maintains that the settlements are legal and argues that the Fourth Geneva Convention does not apply to the West Bank and East Jerusalem, as they were not recognized as sovereign territories prior to Israel's occupation. Israel also cites historical and religious claims to the land and maintains that the settlements are necessary for its security.

The Status of Palestinian Statehood and Recognition

The issue of Palestinian statehood and recognition has been a central component of the Israeli-Palestinian conflict. The Palestinian Authority (PA) has sought recognition as a sovereign state by the international community, but this has been met with resistance from Israel and the United States.

The United Nations General Assembly granted Palestine non-member observer state status in 2012, which allowed it to participate in UN debates and join international treaties. However, Palestine is not recognized as a full member state of the UN, and Israel and the US continue to argue that a negotiated settlement is the only path to Palestinian statehood.

The Applicability of International Humanitarian Law and Human Rights Law

The Israeli-Palestinian conflict is subject to both international humanitarian law and human rights law. International humanitarian law, as set forth in the Fourth Geneva Convention, governs the treatment of civilians and non-combatants in armed conflicts, while human rights law sets out standards for the protection of individual rights and freedoms.

Israel has been accused of numerous violations of international humanitarian law and human rights law in the occupied Palestinian territories, including the use of excessive force against Palestinian civilians, extrajudicial killings, arbitrary detention, and the use of torture.

The Palestinian Authority has also been accused of violating international humanitarian law and human rights law, including the use of violence against Israeli civilians and the failure to protect its own citizens from violence.

The Israeli-Palestinian conflict is a complex issue that involves a range of legal and political considerations. The issue of Israeli settlements in the West Bank and East Jerusalem, the status of Palestinian statehood and recognition, and the applicability of international humanitarian law and human rights law are all important components of the conflict. Despite efforts to resolve the conflict, a lasting solution has yet to be achieved, and the international community continues to work towards a peaceful resolution.

Chapter 4
Humanitarian Impacts of the Conflict

The ongoing conflict in Syria and Palestine has resulted in significant humanitarian impacts on the civilian population. The violence and instability have led to widespread displacement and refugee crises, as well as severe physical and psychological harm to individuals and communities. Humanitarian organizations and aid efforts have played a critical role in providing assistance and support to those affected by the conflict.

Displacement and Refugee Crises in Syria and Palestine

The Syrian conflict, which began in 2011, has resulted in one of the largest refugee crises in modern history. According to the United Nations High Commissioner for Refugees (UNHCR), there are currently over 6.7 million Syrian refugees, with an additional 6.6 million internally displaced persons (IDPs) within Syria. The majority of refugees have fled to neighboring countries, including Turkey, Lebanon, Jordan, Iraq, and Egypt, where they face significant challenges in accessing basic necessities such as food, water, and shelter.

Similarly, the ongoing conflict in Palestine has led to a protracted refugee crisis, with millions of Palestinian refugees spread across the Middle East. The majority of Palestinian refugees are registered with the UN Relief and Works Agency for Palestine Refugees (UNRWA), which provides education, healthcare, and other essential services to refugees in the West Bank, Gaza Strip, Jordan, Lebanon, and Syria.

The Impact of Violence on Civilians

The violence and instability in Syria and Palestine have had severe physical and psychological impacts on civilians, particularly women and children. In Syria, civilians have been subjected to indiscriminate shelling, aerial bombardment, and other forms of violence, resulting in widespread death, injury, and trauma. In addition to the direct physical impacts, the conflict has disrupted critical infrastructure and services, such as healthcare and education, which has further compounded the humanitarian crisis.

Similarly, in Palestine, civilians have faced years of violence and oppression, including military occupation, settler violence, and forced displacement. Palestinian children, in particular, have been subjected to violence and trauma, with high rates of injury and death, as well as mental health problems such as anxiety and post-traumatic stress disorder (PTSD).

The Role of Humanitarian Organizations and Aid Efforts

Humanitarian organizations and aid efforts have played a critical role in providing assistance and support to those affected by the conflict in Syria and Palestine. These organizations provide emergency relief such as food, water, shelter, and medical care to displaced and vulnerable populations, as well as long-term support for recovery and rebuilding.

In Syria, humanitarian organizations such as the UNHCR, the World Food Programme (WFP), and the International Committee of the Red Cross (ICRC) have provided emergency assistance to millions of people affected by the conflict. These organizations work closely with local partners and communities to ensure that aid reaches those who need it most.

Similarly, in Palestine, organizations such as UNRWA and the Palestinian Red Crescent Society (PRCS) provide essential services to Palestinian refugees, including healthcare, education, and emergency relief. These organizations also work to promote human rights, advocate for the protection of civilians, and support community resilience and development.

Despite the critical role of humanitarian organizations and aid efforts, the ongoing conflict and political instability in Syria and Palestine continue to pose significant challenges to their work. Limited access, funding constraints, and security risks can hinder the delivery of aid and support, making it difficult to reach those in need.

In conclusion, the humanitarian impacts of the conflict in Syria and Palestine are significant, with displacement, refugee crises, and violence causing physical and psychological harm to civilians. Humanitarian organizations and aid efforts play a critical role in providing emergency relief and long-term support to those affected by the conflict, but ongoing political instability and insecurity continue to pose significant challenges to their work.

Chapter 5
Prospects for Peace and Reconciliation

After years of conflict and violence, the prospects for peace and reconciliation in the Israeli-Palestinian conflict remain uncertain. However, there are lessons that can be learned from successful peace processes in other conflicts, as well as potential solutions and the role of civil society and grassroots initiatives.

Lessons from successful peace processes in other conflicts

There are numerous examples of successful peace processes in other conflicts that can provide valuable lessons for the Israeli-Palestinian conflict. One of the most significant examples is the Good Friday Agreement in Northern Ireland, which ended decades of sectarian violence between Catholics and Protestants. The agreement was achieved through a combination of political negotiations, grassroots initiatives, and international support. It also included provisions for power-sharing, human rights, and disarmament.

Another example is the peace process in South Africa, which ended apartheid and established a multi-racial democracy. This process was based on a comprehensive reconciliation framework that included truth and reconciliation commissions, reparations for victims, and constitutional reforms.

These examples demonstrate the importance of political negotiations, grassroots initiatives, and international support for achieving peace and reconciliation in a conflict. They also highlight the need for comprehensive frameworks that address the underlying causes of the conflict and provide solutions that are acceptable to all parties.

The potential for a two-state solution

The two-state solution, which envisions the creation of a Palestinian state alongside Israel, has been a central focus of peace negotiations for decades. While the prospects for a two-state solution have been challenged by factors such as settlement expansion and Hamas' control of Gaza, many still view it as the most viable option for resolving the conflict.

Advocates of the two-state solution argue that it would provide a homeland for Palestinians and security for Israelis. It would also allow for the recognition of Palestinian national aspirations and the preservation of Israel's Jewish character.

However, critics of the two-state solution point to obstacles such as the ongoing settlement expansion in the West Bank, which makes it increasingly difficult to establish a contiguous Palestinian state. They also note the continued division between the West Bank and

Gaza, which makes it challenging to create a unified Palestinian state.

Despite these challenges, many policymakers and analysts continue to view the two-state solution as the best option for achieving peace and reconciliation in the region.

The role of civil society and grassroots initiatives

Civil society and grassroots initiatives can play a crucial role in promoting peace and reconciliation in the Israeli-Palestinian conflict. These initiatives can include efforts to build relationships and promote dialogue between Israelis and Palestinians, as well as advocacy for policies and solutions that address the underlying causes of the conflict.

One example of such an initiative is the Parents Circle-Families Forum, which brings together Israeli and Palestinian families who have lost loved ones in the conflict. Through dialogue and shared experiences, these families work to promote understanding and reconciliation.

Other examples include joint Israeli-Palestinian business ventures and cultural exchanges, which help to build trust and relationships between communities.

These initiatives can also complement official peace negotiations by creating momentum and support for peace-building efforts.

Achieving peace and reconciliation in the Israeli-Palestinian conflict remains a daunting challenge, but there are lessons that can be learned from successful peace processes in other conflicts. The potential for a two-state solution remains a central focus of peace negotiations, but there are significant obstacles to its realization. Civil society and grassroots initiatives can play a crucial role in promoting peace and reconciliation by building relationships and promoting understanding between communities.

Summary of key findings

Lessons from successful peace processes in other conflicts can provide valuable insights for resolving the Israeli-Palestinian conflict.

The two-state solution remains the most viable option for achieving peace and reconciliation, despite significant obstacles.

Civil society and grassroots initiatives can play a crucial role in promoting peace and reconciliation by building relationships and promoting understanding between communities.

Implications and recommendations for policymakers and practitioners

Based on the findings discussed above, there are several implications and recommendations for policymakers and practitioners seeking to promote peace and reconciliation in the Israeli-Palestinian conflict.

Firstly, policymakers should draw upon lessons from successful peace processes in other conflicts to inform their approach to resolving the Israeli-Palestinian conflict. This may include exploring innovative solutions that have been successful in other contexts, as well as engaging in dialogue with experts and practitioners who have experience in peace-building.

, policymakers should work to address the underlying causes of the conflict, such as the ongoing occupation of the West Bank and the blockade of Gaza. This may involve supporting economic development and improving access to basic services in Palestinian communities, as well as promoting policies that address the security concerns of both Israelis and Palestinians.

, policymakers should prioritize the role of civil society and grassroots initiatives in promoting peace and reconciliation. This may involve supporting the work of organizations that bring Israelis and Palestinians together to build relationships and promote dialogue, as well as investing in cultural exchanges and joint business ventures.

, policymakers should prioritize the establishment of a comprehensive peace framework that addresses the political, economic, and social dimensions of the conflict. Such a framework should include provisions for power-sharing, human rights, and disarmament, as well as a plan for the establishment of a Palestinian state alongside Israel.

Future research directions

There are several areas in which future research could contribute to the field of peace-building and conflict resolution in the Israeli-Palestinian context. These may include:

Investigating the impact of civil society and grassroots initiatives on peace-building efforts.

Examining the role of external actors, such as the United States and the European Union, in promoting peace and reconciliation.

Analyzing the impact of settlement expansion and other obstacles to the two-state solution on the prospects for peace and reconciliation.

Investigating the feasibility of alternative solutions, such as a single-state solution or a confederation.

Examining the role of media and communication in shaping public attitudes towards the conflict and peace-building efforts.

Overall, there is a great deal of work that remains to be done to achieve lasting peace and reconciliation in the Israeli-Palestinian conflict. However, by drawing upon lessons from successful peace processes in other conflicts, prioritizing civil society and grassroots initiatives, and investing in comprehensive peace frameworks, policymakers and practitioners can work towards a more peaceful and prosperous future for Israelis and Palestinians alike.

REFERENCES

Galtung, J. (2002). Conflict transformation by peaceful means (the Transcend method). Geneva Centre for Security Policy.

Johnson, R. (2016). The Good Friday Agreement and peace process in Northern Ireland. International Affairs Review, 24(1), 20-33.

Lederach, J. P. (2003). The little book of conflict transformation: Clear articulation of the guiding principles by a pioneer in the field. Good Books.

Sisk, T. D. (2018). Good Friday Agreement, Northern Ireland. Oxford Research Encyclopedia of Politics.

United Nations. (2015). Report of the United Nations Secretary-General on the implementation of Security Council resolution 1701 (2006). United Nations.

United Nations Development Programme. (2014). Arab Human Development Report 2014: Youth and the Prospects for Human Development in a Changing Reality. United Nations Development Programme.

United Nations Office on Drugs and Crime. (2016). International drug control and human rights: A brief overview. United Nations Office on Drugs and Crime.

United States Institute of Peace. (2015). USIP Peace Brief: Lessons from International Peacebuilding. United States Institute of Peace.

Weller, M. (2015). Peace process in Northern Ireland. Oxford Research Encyclopedia of Politics.

These resources provide valuable insights into the challenges and opportunities for peace-building in the Israeli-Palestinian conflict.

Policymakers and practitioners can draw upon these resources to inform their approach to resolving the conflict and promoting lasting peace and reconciliation.